1 PIANO, 4 HANDS

PIANO
DUET
PLAY-ALONG

VOLUME 29

BROADWAY CLASSICS

ISBN 978-1-4234-6137-1

HAL•LEONARD®
CORPORATION
7777 W. BLUEMOUND RD. P.O.BOX 13819 MILWAUKEE, WI 53213

Visit Hal Leonard Online at
www.halleonard.com

CONTENTS

CAN'T HELP LOVIN' DAT MAN

from SHOW BOAT

SECONDO

Lyrics by OSCAR HAMMERSTEIN II
Music by JEROME KERN

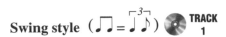

CAN'T HELP LOVIN' DAT MAN

from SHOW BOAT

PRIMO

Lyrics by OSCAR HAMMERSTEIN II
Music by JEROME KERN

SECONDO

DON'T CRY FOR ME ARGENTINA

from EVITA

SECONDO

Words by TIM RICE
Music by ANDREW LLOYD WEBBER

Expressively TRACK 3

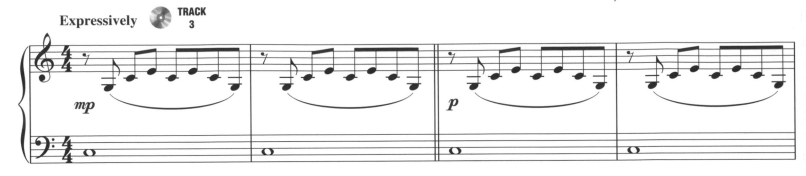

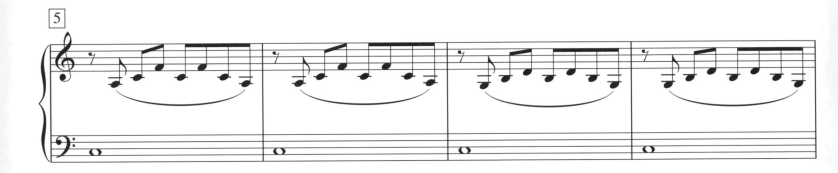

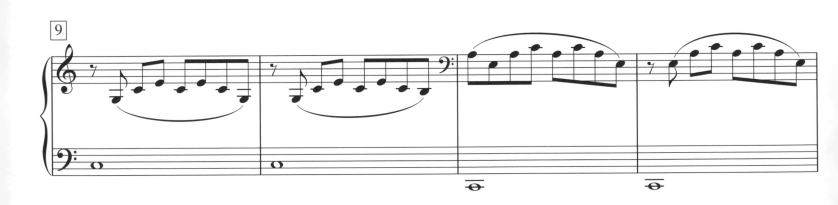

DON'T CRY FOR ME ARGENTINA

from EVITA

PRIMO

Words by TIM RICE
Music by ANDREW LLOYD WEBBER

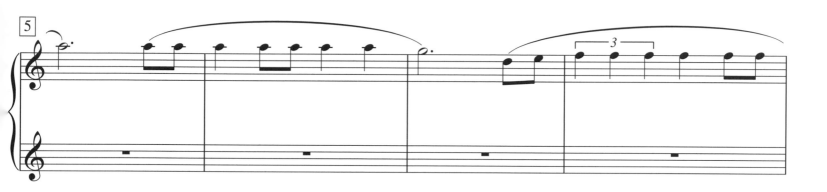

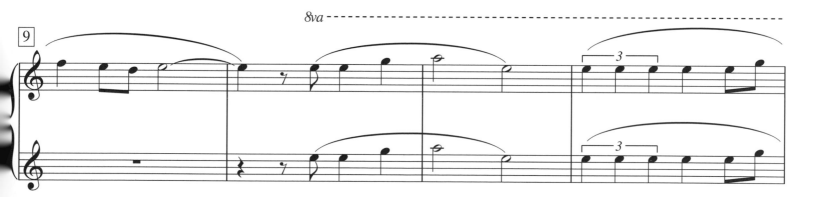

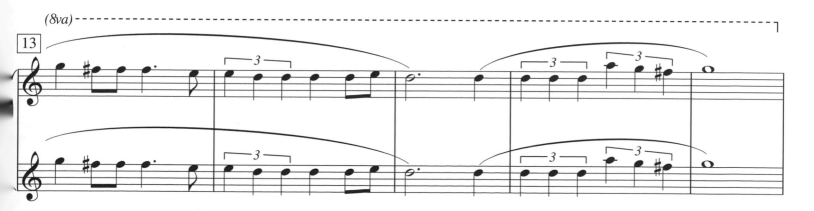

SECONDO

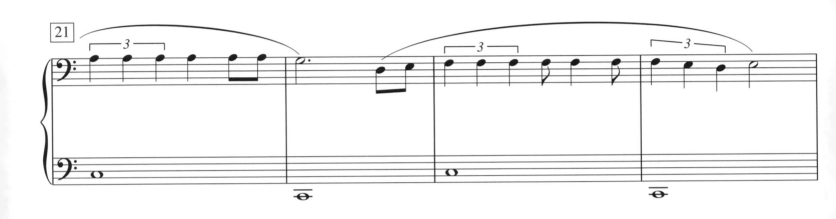

PRIMO

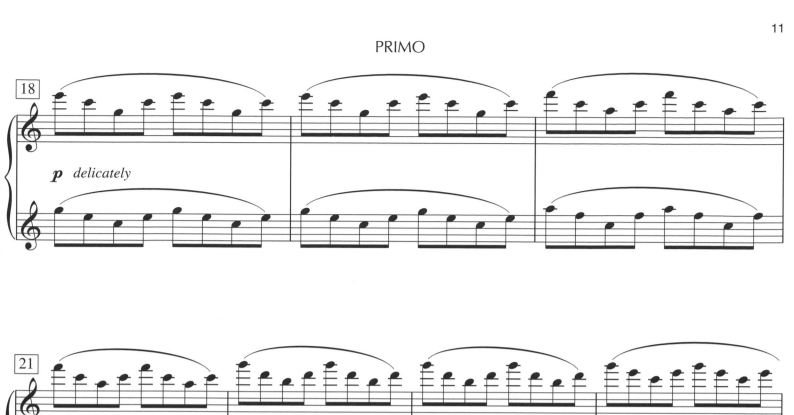

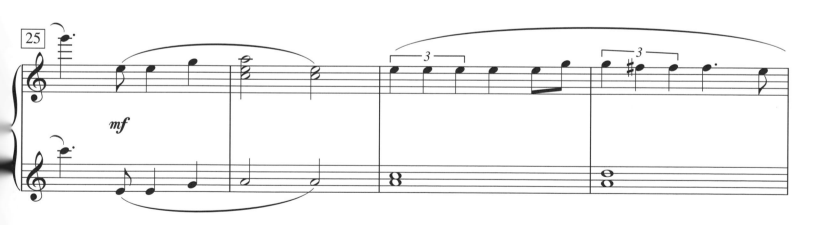

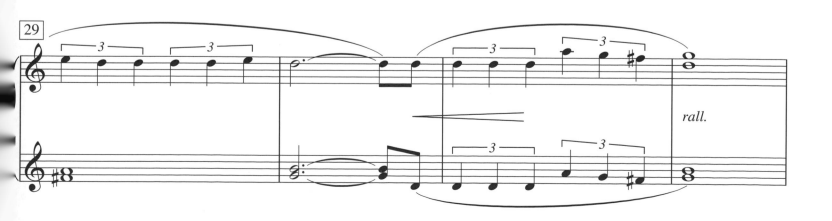

SECONDO

PRIMO

SECONDO

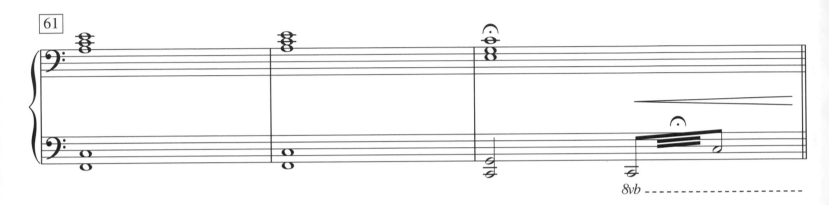

PRIMO

HELLO, DOLLY!

from HELLO, DOLLY!

SECONDO

Music and Lyric by
JERRY HERMAN

Medium Strut (♩ = ca. 72) TRACK 5

HELLO, DOLLY!

from HELLO, DOLLY!

PRIMO

Music and Lyric by
JERRY HERMAN

SECONDO

SECONDO

SECONDO

PRIMO

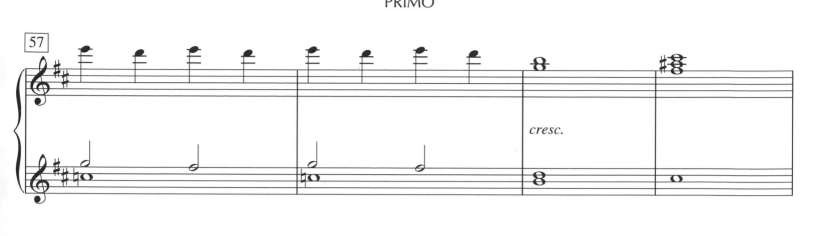

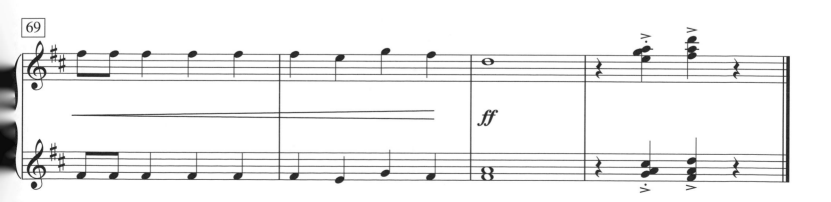

IT MIGHT AS WELL BE SPRING

from STATE FAIR

SECONDO

Lyrics by OSCAR HAMMERSTEIN II
Music by RICHARD RODGERS

Gracefully (♩ = ca. 100) TRACK 7

IT MIGHT AS WELL BE SPRING
from STATE FAIR

PRIMO

Lyrics by OSCAR HAMMERSTEIN II
Music by RICHARD RODGERS

Gracefully ($\quarternote$ = ca. 100) TRACK 8

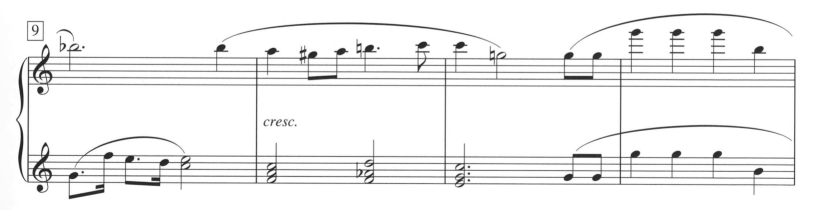

SECONDO

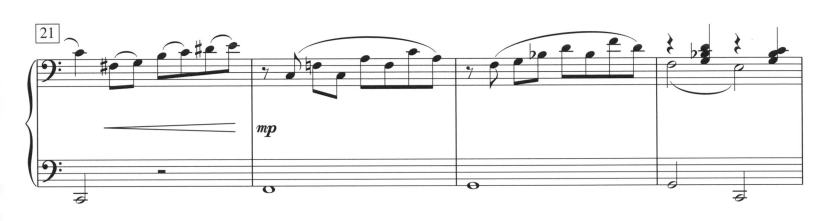

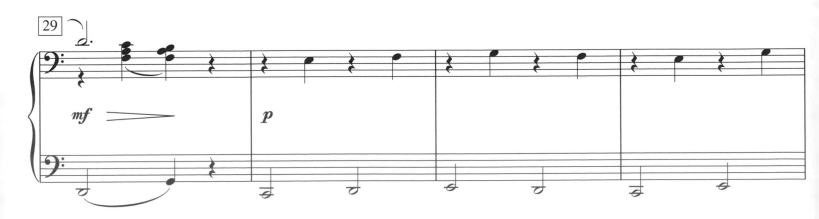

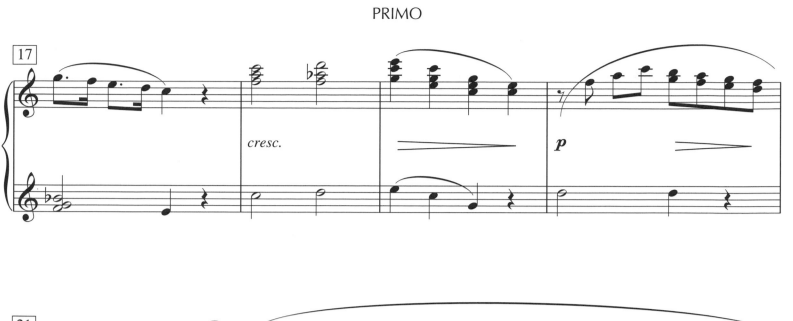

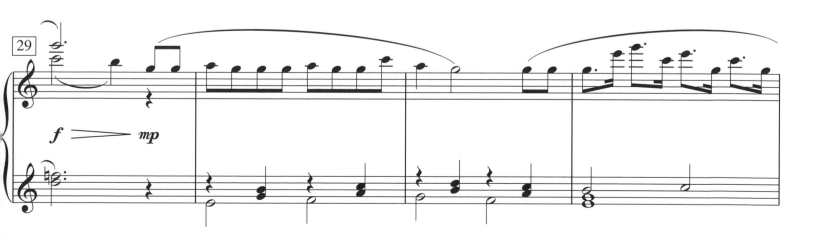

SECONDO

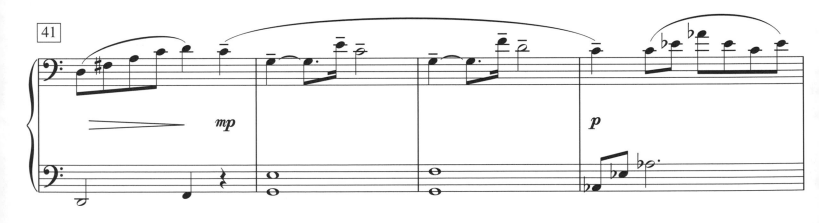

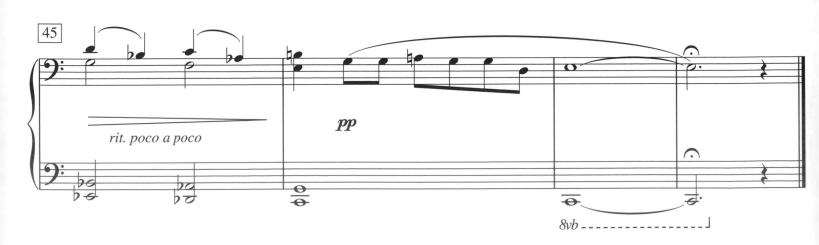

PRIMO

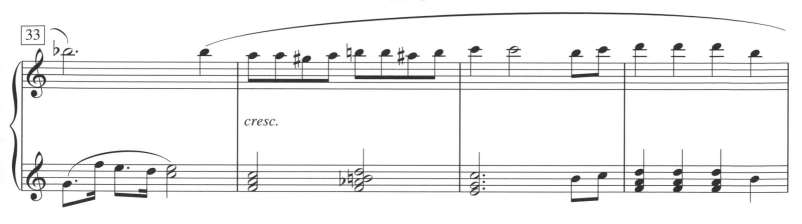

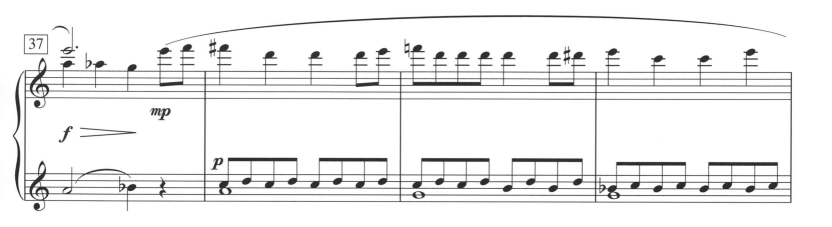

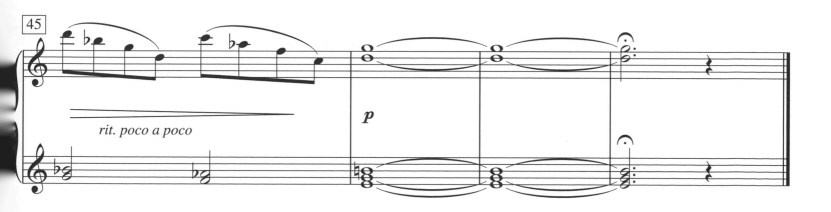

LUCK BE A LADY
from GUYS AND DOLLS

SECONDO

By FRANK LOESSER

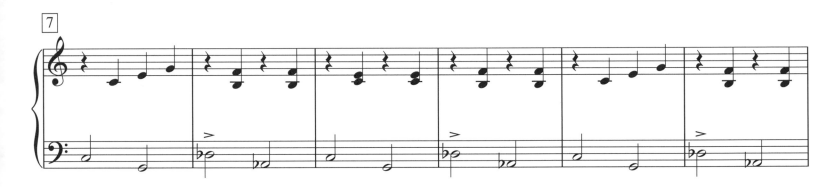

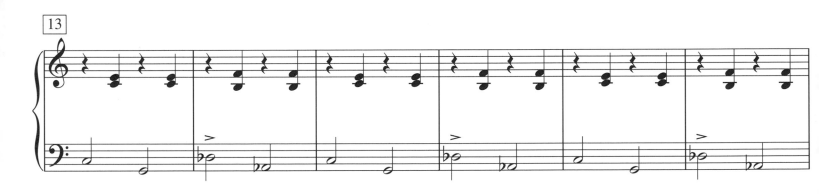

LUCK BE A LADY
from GUYS AND DOLLS

PRIMO

By FRANK LOESSER

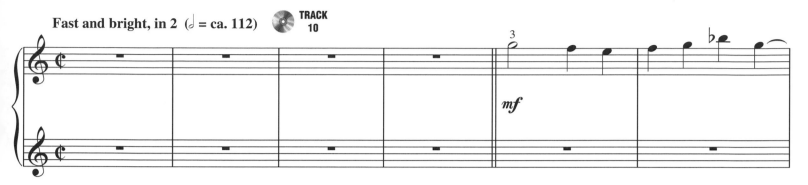

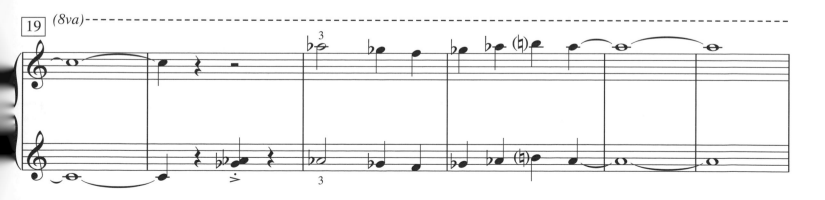

SECONDO

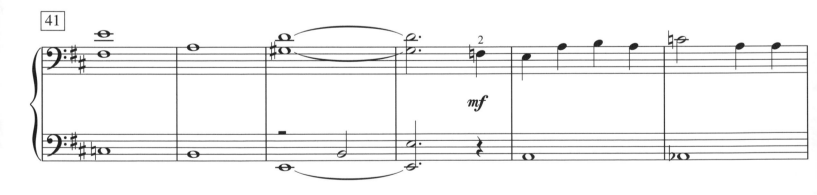

SECONDO

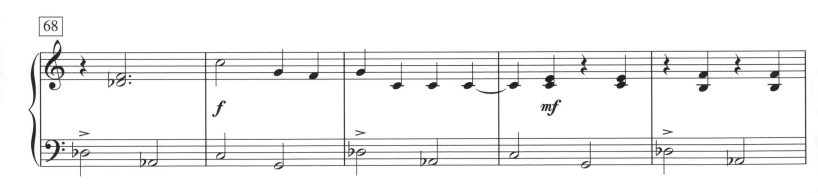

PRIMO

OH, WHAT A BEAUTIFUL MORNIN'

from OKLAHOMA!

SECONDO

Lyrics by OSCAR HAMMERSTEIN II
Music by RICHARD RODGERS

Moderate Waltz tempo (♩ = ca. 144)　TRACK 11

OH, WHAT A BEAUTIFUL MORNIN'
from OKLAHOMA!

PRIMO

Lyrics by OSCAR HAMMERSTEIN II
Music by RICHARD RODGERS

Moderate Waltz tempo (♩ = ca. 144) TRACK 12

SECONDO

SECONDO

PRIMO

ONE

from A CHORUS LINE

SECONDO

Music by MARVIN HAMLISCH
Lyric by EDWARD KLEBAN

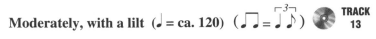

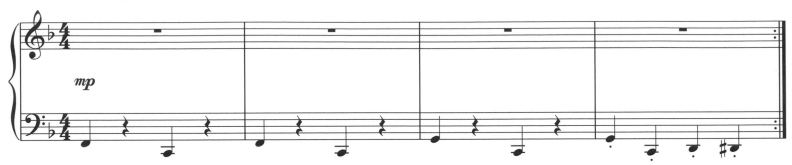

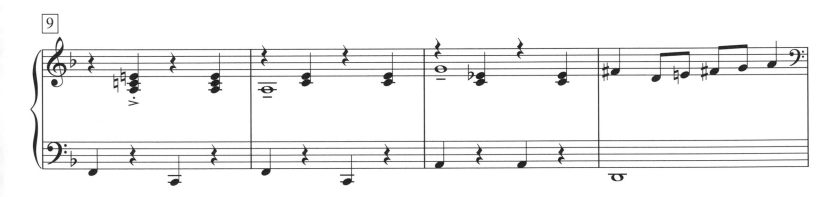

ONE
from A CHORUS LINE

PRIMO

Music by MARVIN HAMLISCH
Lyric by EDWARD KLEBAN

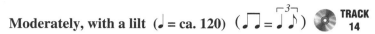

Moderately, with a lilt (♩ = ca. 120)

SECONDO

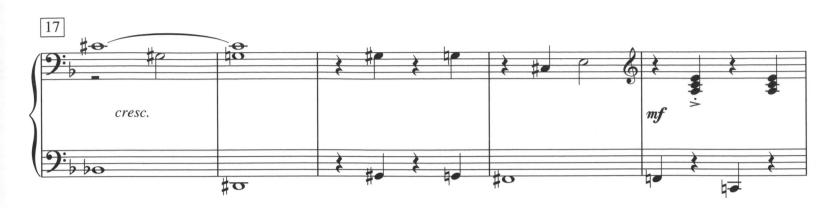

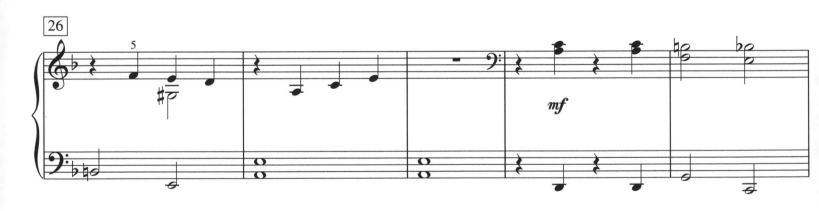

PRIMO

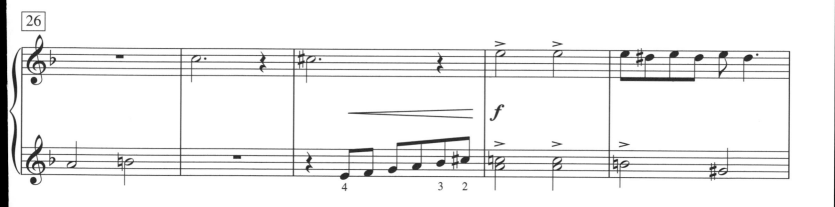

SECONDO

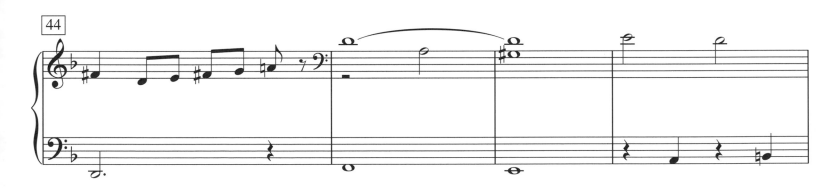

PRIMO

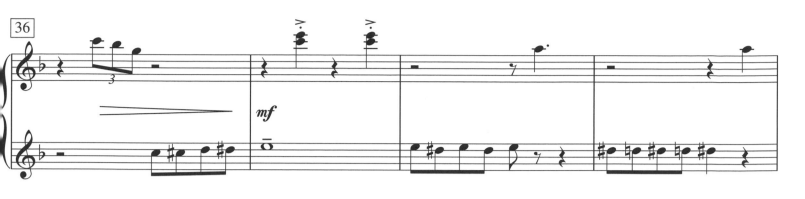

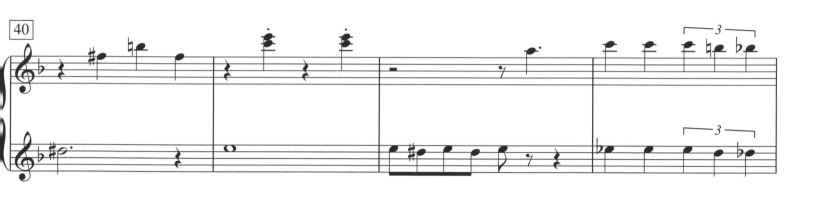

SECONDO

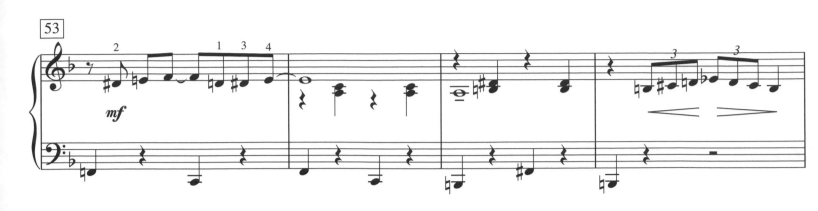

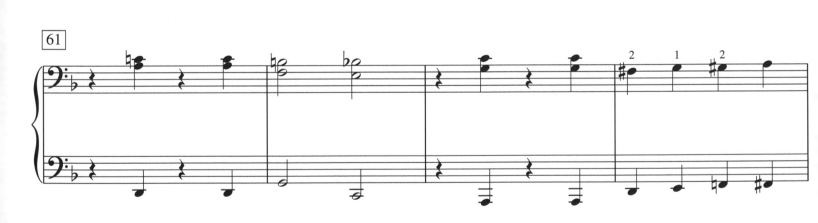

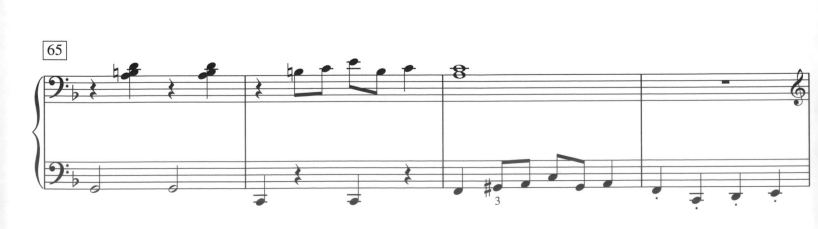

PRIMO

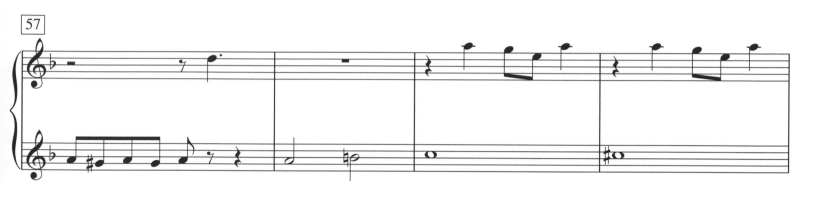

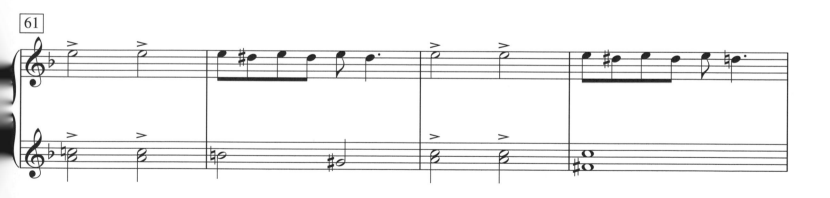

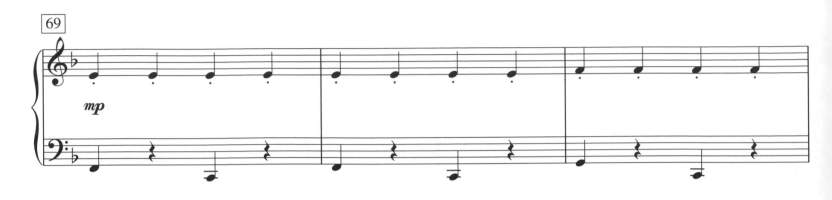

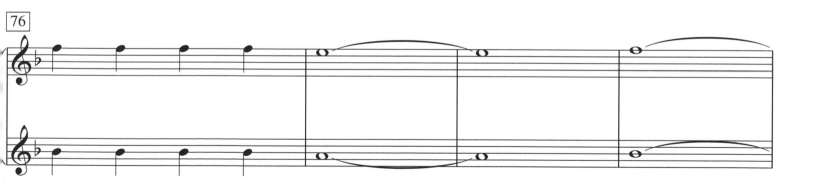

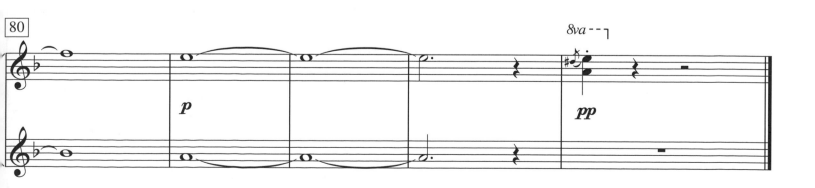

TOMORROW
from the Musical Production ANNIE

SECONDO

Lyric by MARTIN CHARNIN
Music by CHARLES STROUSE

Moderately, with a lilt · TRACK 15

TOMORROW
from the Musical Production ANNIE

PRIMO

Lyric by MARTIN CHARNIN
Music by CHARLES STROUSE

Moderately, with a lilt TRACK 16

SECONDO

PIANO DUET PLAY-ALONG

The **Piano Duet Play-Along** series gives you the flexibility to rehearse or perform piano duets anytime, anywhere! Play these delightful tunes with a partner, or use the accompanying CDs to play along with either the Secondo or Primo part on your own. The CD is playable on any CD player, and also enhanced so PC and Mac users can adjust the recording to any tempo without changing pitch.